DATE DUE

ART FROM HER HEART

FOLK ARTIST CLEMENTINE HUNTER

KATHY WHITEHEAD

SHANE W. EVANS

G. P. PUTNAM'S SONS

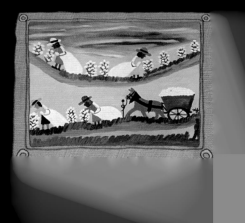

Clementine waited until her work in the Big House was done and the twinkle of stars filled the night sky above the Cane River. She was ready to paint, like the artists she cooked and cleaned for on Melrose Plantation.

But she didn't wait for the perfect set of paints and canvas. She used the leftovers the artists gave her. Instead of canvas, she used window shades, glass bottles, black iron skillets, and old boards— whatever she could find.

In the middle of her hundred years, Clementine Hunter had decided to paint.

No one gave her lessons. As a girl, she had never even learned to read or write. Clementine didn't like school and soon quit. She told her mama she'd rather pick cotton.

She was the oldest but the smallest of her six brothers and
sisters. Her nickname was Tebé (Tee-bay), from the French words
for "little baby."

She called herself Clementine when she was old enough to pick flowers and haul them home in a cart.

When Clementine decided to paint pictures, she didn't wait for the perfect art studio. While everyone was sleeping, she created bright-colored images in the dim kerosene light of her small cabin.

She didn't wait to travel and seek inspiration in foreign lands. She drew the pictures in her memory—scenes of life on Melrose Plantation. Clementine thought back to days of dragging a hundred-pound sack of cotton down endless rows while her children sat under a tree in the field.

Memories of picking pecans in the fall in the big pecan groves, to make extra money.

She remembered wash days
spent over black wash pots and
clothes flapping on a clothes-
line. Long days of hard work
and little pay.

There were good times on the plantation, and Clementine recorded them also.

Couples laughing and dancing on a Saturday night, like the dance where Clementine met her husband, Emmanuel.

Simple joys like
scattering feed to
a flock of hungry
chickens.

Fishing for catfish and bream with a cane pole on the Cane River, to cook at a fish fry. Clementine enjoyed fishing at the river with her grandson, but she always fished from the bank. She didn't like getting in boats.

Clementine painted special times on
the plantation too. Pictures of a couple on
their wedding day.

Graduates waiting in line for their diplomas,
a paper that Clementine didn't receive
until the end of her years.

And children in white robes ready for
their baptism in the Cane River. Her
grandchildren walked into the water for their
baptism, happy days that Clementine loved to paint.

Clementine didn't wait for the world to find her art. She hung a
sign on her gate that read "Art Exhibit. Admission 25¢. Thanks."

People came to see her pictures pinned on a clothes-
line, and bought them. Friends who recognized her talent
gave her paints, paper, and brushes. They helped her find
galleries that would display and sell her work.

Years later, people lined up to see her artwork
at a big museum in New Orleans, Louisiana.

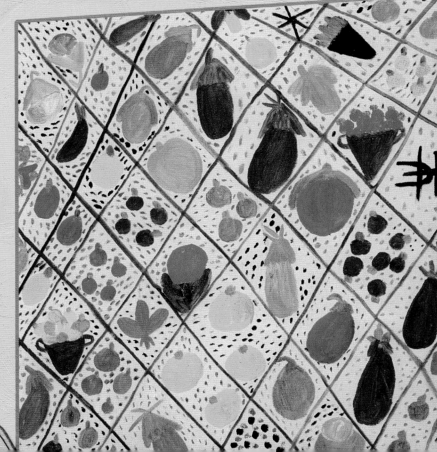

Clementin
Hunter

Another gallery proudly displayed her work but refused to let
her in the front door. She had to wait until after hours to enjoy
her own pictures on display. But the laws that kept her out would
soon be gone like feed thrown to the chickens.

The art that poured from Clementine's heart and mind gives us a window to her life on the plantation. A window we would have missed if Clementine Hunter had waited for the perfect time to paint.

Hog Killin', painted 1950, oil on board.

Zinnias in a Yellow Pot,
painted 1950, oil on masonite.

Pickin' & Haulin Cotton, painted
1950, oil on board.

Gourds, painted about 1950,
oil on paperboard.

Thomas N. Whitehead Collection

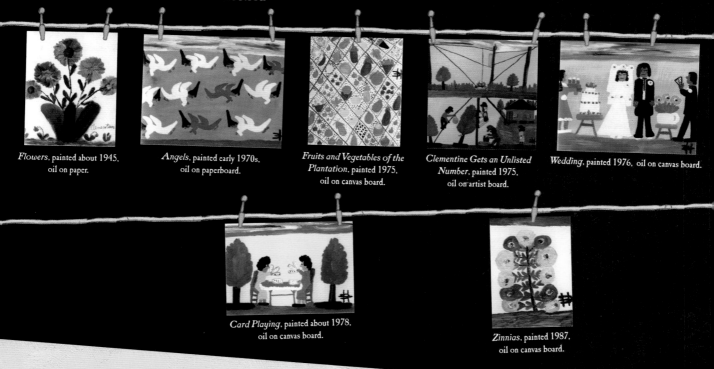

Flowers, painted about 1945,
oil on paper.

Angels, painted early 1970s,
oil on paperboard.

*Fruits and Vegetables of the
Plantation*, painted 1975,
oil on canvas board.

*Clementine Gets an Unlisted
Number*, painted 1975,
oil on artist board.

Wedding, painted 1976, oil on canvas board.

Card Playing, painted about 1978,
oil on canvas board.

Zinnias, painted 1987,
oil on canvas board.

BIBLIOGRAPHY

Gilley, Shelby R. *Painting by Heart: The Life and Art of Clementine Hunter,
Louisiana Folk Artist.* Baton Rouge, La.: St. Emma Press, 2000.

Lyons, Mary E., editor. *Talking with Tebé—Clementine Hunter, Memory Artist.* Boston, Mass.: Houghton Mifflin, 1998.

Shiver, Art, and Tom Whitehead, editors. *Clementine Hunter: The African House Murals.* Natchitoches, La.:
Northwestern State University Press, 2005.

Wilson, James L. *Clementine Hunter: American Folk Artist.* Gretna, La.: Pelican, 1988.

AUTHOR'S NOTE

Clementine (pronounced "Clementeen") Hunter was born in Natchitoches Parish, Louisiana, in December 1886 or early January 1887. A descendant of slaves, she worked as a manual laborer on a plantation. She did various jobs such as picking cotton, harvesting pecans, and kitchen work.

She lived on Melrose Plantation, which was owned by Mrs. Cammie Henry. Melrose was a haven for well-known artists and writers. One of the writers, François Mignon, became aware of Hunter's desire to paint when she asked to use some tubes of paint left behind by visiting artist Alberta Kinsey. Mignon found a brush and an old window shade to use as a canvas, and the next morning Hunter brought her finished painting for him to view. He was delighted with her efforts. Later, he introduced her to James Pipes Register. Register recognized the unique character of her work and joined Mignon in providing materials, funds, and support for her artistic growth.

When she first began to paint, Hunter sold her artwork for twenty-five cents each, but she was hesitant to charge even that. She preferred giving pieces away since she felt she might be cheating people by taking money for her works. As her artistic reputation grew, Mignon and Register assisted Hunter in selling and promoting her work. She became more well-known and the price of her artwork rose: three dollars apiece in the early 1960s, hundreds of dollars in the 1970s, and finally thousands of dollars each in the 1980s.

Hunter's work spanned several decades, illuminating the world she had been born into. She documented scenes of the labor-intensive farm life that she experienced firsthand prior to the changes brought about by the Second World War. Her large murals for the African House, a two-story Congo-style hut on Melrose, are considered a national treasure for their telling of the story of everyday life and celebrations on the plantation.

Clementine Hunter was the first self-taught African-American woman artist to capture the attention of the national media at a time when segregation laws kept her from attending her own gallery shows. In 1955 the Delgado Museum (now the New Orleans Museum of Art) presented a Hunter exhibition, its first for an African-American artist. That same year, Northwestern State College in Natchitoches held an exhibit of Hunter's work. Hunter was not allowed to attend the exhibition during normal hours with the white patrons. Instead, a friend took her through the back door on a Sunday when the gallery was closed.

She received an Honorary Doctorate of Fine Arts from Northwestern State University, Natchitoches, Louisiana, in 1986. Her pictures are sold in galleries across the country and are on permanent display in many museums. She painted until her last days and was pleased with the independence it gave her. Clementine Hunter died January 1, 1988.

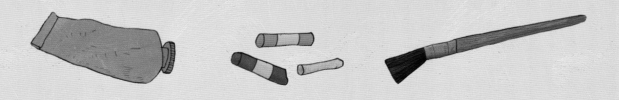

To my wonderful parents, Steve and Jean. —K. W.

Thank you, God. This book is dedicated to my parents, Jackie Evans and Marie Askin—thank you for helping to nurture my gifts. —S. E.

ACKNOWLEDGMENTS

I give my wholehearted thanks to Tom Whitehead and the Brittain family for their help, time, and generosity with their collections. The following people also generously provided help along the way: Ann Dorer; Iris Harper; Shelby R. Gilley; the Frederick R. Weisman Art Museum, Minneapolis, Minnesota; the Louisiana State Museum, New Orleans, Louisiana; and Melrose Plantation, Natchitoches, Louisiana.

Special thanks to my husband, Bill, my family, and my friends for their encouragement and support throughout the many steps of this book's progress. Thanks to Janet Fox, Shirley Hoskins, and Kathi Appelt for their ongoing assistance.

I am grateful to my editor, Susan Kochan, for her invaluable wisdom and support.

—Kathy Whitehead

G. P. PUTNAM'S SONS
A division of Penguin Young Readers Group.
Published by The Penguin Group.
Penguin Group (USA) Inc., 375 Hudson Street, New York, NY 10014, U.S.A.
Penguin Group (Canada), 90 Eglinton Avenue East, Suite 700, Toronto, Ontario M4P 2Y3, Canada (a division of Pearson Penguin Canada Inc.).
Penguin Books Ltd, 80 Strand, London WC2R 0RL, England.
Penguin Ireland, 25 St. Stephen's Green, Dublin 2, Ireland (a division of Penguin Books Ltd.).
Penguin Group (Australia), 250 Camberwell Road, Camberwell, Victoria 3124, Australia (a division of Pearson Australia Group Pty Ltd).
Penguin Books India Pvt Ltd, 11 Community Centre, Panchsheel Park, New Delhi - 110 017, India.
Penguin Group (NZ), 67 Apollo Drive, Rosedale, North Shore 0632, New Zealand (a division of Pearson New Zealand Ltd).
Penguin Books (South Africa) (Pty) Ltd, 24 Sturdee Avenue, Rosebank, Johannesburg 2196, South Africa.
Penguin Books Ltd, Registered Offices: 80 Strand, London WC2R 0RL, England.

Library of Congress Cataloging-in-Publication Data
Whitehead, Kathy. Art from her heart : folk artist Clementine Hunter / Kathy Whitehead ; illustrated by Shane Evans.   p. cm.
1. Hunter, Clementine—Juvenile literature. 2. African American painters—Louisiana—Biography—Juvenile literature. 3. Folk artists—Louisiana—Biography—Juvenile literature. 4. Plantations in art—Juvenile literature.
I. Evans, Shane. II. Title.   ND237.H915W45 2008   759.13—dc22   [B] 2006034458

ISBN 978-0-399-24219-9

10 9 8 7 6 5 4